Wisdom, Wit, and Whimsy:

Quips That Empower, Enlighten, and Entertain

Lisa L. Nokes

ISBN: 0998051403
ISBN-13: 978-0-9980514-0-6

Cover Photo Credit:

Amanda J. M. Nokes

DEDICATION

Hi, MOM! This one is for you. You've always had so much faith in me, even when I have none in myself. You have been my best friend, my biggest cheerleader, my fan club president, and bodyguard. I love you more than words can adequately express. I am so happy that you can see one of my dreams become a reality Oh, and here is your name officially in print:
JOYCE SCHLINGLOFF!!
Thank you! All my love!

To my amazing daughter, Amanda. You are a joy every day. How fortunate I am to be your mom and to know you as a person. I am so proud of you and cannot wait to see where life takes you (as long as it is not more than 30 miles from me. HA!).

Troy, my husband, GLOML. You have kept my heart safe and my mind sane. Our relationship is everything I hoped it would be when we reconnected, and so much more than I ever imagined when we went to high school together all those years ago. What clarity you bring to my life. Thank you for supporting me, and for genuinely being excited for me to pursue my dreams. My life is more full, fun, and just plain "more" because you are part of it.

Dad, Robert Brewer, I love you! Thank you for always believing in me and encouraging me in every endeavor. Your love of books got me interested in reading at an early age. Even now with digital downloads, and audio books, I still enjoy holding a book in my hands.

To Karen Matteson, my BFFLMNOP, I am so grateful to have you in my life my 2 o'clock in the morning friend. We have been through so much together. What amazing memories we have, with more to be made as we continue filming episodes of The Karen & Lisa Show! Give me those rocking chairs girl!

To a friend who feels more like family every day, Stacy Jo Hartley. I am so glad our paths crossed. You welcomed not only my daughter but me, with open arms and heart. You have such a warm spirit and compassionate heart. You get my sense of humor because yours is shockingly similar (a rare find)! So glad to have someone so amazing and special in my life.

(Auntie) Kathy Nokes, thank you for always being such a cheerleader for our family. Thank you also for volunteering your services to edit this "dream turned reality" of a book. Disclaimer: I may have added some things after you finished editing. Oops.

Lastly, to Stevie Chao. A co-worker, friend, and future President of the United States. Thank you for helping me noodle around book titles until the perfect one came together.

INTRODUCTION

Are you the person who wonders why me, or the one who says why not me? Are you the one who walks with a bounce in your step and is always looking for the rainbow after the storm; or, do you just want to punch that person in the throat?

Do you ever wonder why some people seem to be able to find happiness no matter how bleak their circumstances; and others, they can find a way to be bleak no matter how happy their circumstances?

Are you sick of hearing that it's all a matter of perspective, but secretly believe that it probably really is all a matter of perspective? (Turn to pages 24, 49 and 80 for my thoughts on that.)

Whether you are sure that everything happens for a reason, or you are just sure that everything happens period, this book is for you.
This book is a no holds barred; no punches pulled, "tell it like it is" challenge to the way you look at life.

There is a good deal of silliness and a whole lot of truth. You will probably laugh; you may even cry, but you will most definitely think.

Bonus! Increase your confidence and improve your outlook in just 5 minutes a day using proven Mindset Mini Mantras. My gift to you at: www.wisdomwitandwhimsy.com/bookbonus

Why are you still in the introduction?
Turn the page and let's get started!!!

Making change takes minor math skills. *Being* change takes major life skills.

Sometimes we need to stop all the running and doing, and focus on the living and being. Life is about experiences, not errands.

It is not how we agree that is the best indicator of our compatibility as friends or lovers. Rather, it is how we disagree.

I am not nearly as interested in what you stand against, as I am in what you stand for.

They say if you want your fairytale ending you have to kiss a few frogs. I say, "Nah, you just have to throat punch a few evil doers."

The famous Beatles song says, "All you need is love." I would add "and the courage to stand for love in the face of hate."

When we view the world through a lens of "us against them" – we create a world of "us against us."

Stuff happens.

Things change.

Circumstances beyond our control find ways to impact us.

At the end of the day, if the people (or animals, plants, furniture, etc.) waiting for us to get home are happier because we are there, it's all good.

Being the bigger person can be painful. You should see the holes in my tongue from all the biting!

When the writing is on the wall, it is good to be literate!

If you are going out on a limb, make sure it is a sturdy one. Nothing is worse than trying to stand on your principles, only to fall on your face.

In trying times, it is important that you keep trying!

You cannot expect others to realize that you can't do it all if you have not yet figured that out yourself.

Find your bliss. When you know why you are happy, then your circumstances cannot make you "not OK." They may frustrate you, but they do not change you. Only you can do that.

At the end of the day, if I do not matter to you, your opinion does not matter to me.

Recycling the words of my bfflmnop (sorry, top secret code - can't decode it for you, but it is super cool that it's in a book, right?):

Sometimes, when it feels like your life has come to a screeching halt, you want to hit the "fast forward" button to a year from now, the other side, beyond the pain.

But you have to live through each of the 365 days it takes to get to a year from now. It is only then that you will find yourself stronger, happier, healthier and perhaps even unrecognizable in comparison to who you are right now.

I am thankful that I have finally learned how to choose who/what I will allow in my life, without guilt. While I would never intentionally upset someone, I no longer make choices for myself that make me uncomfortable rather than allowing someone else to be uncomfortable. Life is much more fulfilling when you live it, rather than manage it (or worse still, just survive it).

For something to be lost, I have to want to find it. Otherwise, it is simply something that is gone.

At least you can lead a horse to water. A stubborn ass on the other hand ...

Why is there a P-trap in the sink? It seems only the toilet should need one. Just sayin'.

The test of true happiness is whether someone else can take it away. Sadly, those who cannot find happiness often seem to take great delight in trying to steal it from others.

When faced with a sore loser, it is important to be a gracious winner.

I do not desire to be invisible; however, I do not need to make a show of my presence. It is not necessary for me to be in the spotlight to feel as though I have made a mark in the world. Instead, I choose to leave a mark on the people in my part of the world. They, in turn, will leave a mark on the people in their part of the world. So on, and on, until I have indeed made a mark in the world.

Upon asking a chicken why it was crossing the road, it looked at us as if to say, "Isn't it obvious?" Yes, that happened.

Procrastination robs you of peace. It often takes more time and effort than doing the thing you are trying so desperately to avoid.

I have realized that the things that drive me crazy are the very things that keep me sane!

Sometimes, to make room for the good you deserve in your life, you must be willing to let go of the negative you have been allowing to occupy its space.

Do all your relationships end poorly? Do you find that you are never able to catch a break at work? Are you always doing for others but don't feel like anybody does for you? If the answer to these questions is yes, recognize that the common denominator is **you**. You can't whine and "victim" yourself into a different set of circumstances. You will need to put in a little effort.

If you prefer the victim role, at least have enough clarity to recognize that you are living the life you choose/create.

If, however, you want something more – something better, you need only choose to begin to change.

Ever notice that often when people apologize for a misunderstanding, their demeanor clearly implies that it was you who misunderstood? Somehow, it does not occur to them that perhaps they misspoke or failed to clearly make their point.

Perhaps the best response in these instances would be, "apology accepted."

One of the most predictable things about predictable people is that they think they are unpredictable.

Miserable people are, by definition, miserable people.

I once believed that if one could sleep soundly at night, it was a good day. I have since realized that some people use sleep aids, and others have no conscience.

If you want people to respect your opinion, respect them when you share it.

I find it interesting when people are guilty of the very behavior they complain about in others and fail to see the irony.

Sometimes the only part of your circumstance that you can change is you.

I have heard it said, "You only hurt the ones you love." I think a more accurate statement is, "You can only hurt the ones who love you."

Doing something *for* me is not the same as doing something *to* you.

Sometimes, the person who is the rock you lean on needs for you to be the rock.

What I intend often has no bearing on other people's perception of the situation.

It is a talented liar who believes his own lies.

Never turn your back on a backstabber. (Quoting the best mom EVAH.)

Sometimes your best is not good enough for others, but it should always be good enough for you. Keep in mind that most people hold others to a standard they themselves are not capable of reaching.

Revisionist History: A practice allowing you to always be right.

How you treat me speaks far more of your character than it does of mine.

The landscape remained the same as you climbed from the valley to the mountaintop. The only thing that changed was your perspective.

What another person does is on them. My response? That's on me.

My opinion most definitely matters, it just may not matter to everyone. I am learning to be OK with that.

Those who would have me believe my dreams are foolish and unattainable are the same ones who lack the confidence to pursue their own.

I do not ask that you agree with me, just be honest with me. I can handle a difference in opinion. I cannot handle deceit. My mother always said, "You know a thief will steal from you, but you have no idea the damage a liar will do." (That was a nugget mom.)

It is not that I won't allow for the possibility that you will change, it's just that I am no longer holding my breath.

You find out a lot about a person when you dare to disagree.

You cannot teach the person who listens only to his voice. (Paraphrased from the best mom EVAH.)

No matter how old they get, some people never grow beyond being the schoolyard bully.

The absence of emotion is every bit as telling as anger or contempt, perhaps even more so.

Giving up control can be very liberating. It can also be frustrating as heck!

I do not state a differing opinion as a result of not caring what you think … rather, I state it as a result of equally valuing what I think.

"If Only" is not a place; therefore, it is not a destination I can reach.

I cannot control the destructive choices of others, but I can put myself outside the blast radius.

If you find yourself in relationship "management" mode whenever you are relating to certain people, it is not a true relationship.

When you are comfortable with who you are, you are not threatened by who anyone else is.

When you invite people to your pity party, do not hold your breath waiting for RSVPs.

It often takes a painful trip down the wrong path to recognize the right one.

Some people are so busy being the victim that they fail to see how they victimize others.

If the world seems to be always conspiring against you, the chances are that you are conspiring against yourself.

A good measure of the quality of your life: When left alone with your thoughts, is there more laughter than tears?

The opposite of love is not hate; it is the absence of love.

I am not certain I believe that when a door closes, you should look for a window. Sometimes a little bit of patience will change what is on the other side of the door, and that can be a good thing.

Smile like you mean it, you will soon find that you do.

Unconditional love is not blind; rather, it exists despite what it sees.

Any sentence begun by your 15-year-old with the words, "I was watching a documentary the other day…" is going to end well, no matter what!

It is wonderful when the people closest to you are the very people you want close to you.

No need to wait for the machines to rise like a scene from a movie. When you allow others to do your thinking, you give up a key piece of your humanity.

I am often astounded by the arrogance of those who feign humility.

When your heart is full of love and your life is full of laughter, you can more easily handle the days when your pockets are not full of money.

Some mysteries are not meant to be solved. To that end, I shall henceforth be known as: "Missed Serious."

When you give someone the silent treatment, you are saying far more than you realize.

He who sings his own praises is likely performing a solo.

Love -- more than sentiments you can write on a card, more than saying the word can express, more than a newly infatuated couple can comprehend, and more than an aged married couple can describe.

Love is the thing that allows us to feel pain so deeply that we think we cannot withstand it and simultaneously begins to put our broken hearts back together. Do not love in secret. Love is the best "show and tell" EVER!

Now and then I have to dream new dreams – because the ones I dreamed before have all come true.

There was anger - and pain
There was contempt - there was blame
Shaking of fists at the heavens above

There was fear - and regret
There was so much and yet
With all there was, there still wasn't love

There was freedom - and peace
There was growth - and release
Finally finding a love that is true

Now there's laughter and fun
There's no doubt you're the one
I love spending forever with you

Hatred and ignorance are easy choices. It takes the strength of character to seek knowledge and informed opinions that are arrived at through contemplation, rather than dictation.

I refuse to be what I am not, just to make you OK with what you are.

Your failure to rise to the occasion will not cause me to stoop to your level.

Too often life is lived in such a way that we are surprised when things go right, rather than when they go wrong.

If I were writing my fairy tale ending, it would read, "and then her eyes lit up, with a smile that started deep within."

"Dear Trick or Treaters: We are the house giving out dental floss. Spread the word." (Thank you, Amanda)

If you stretch a dollar far enough, do zeros start to appear?

The feeling you get when you plan to call your crush and ask him/her out on a date, and then you get the butterflies of anticipation. Yeah, I really like that feeling.

When it is always someone else's fault, it is probably your fault.

As long as you are a student, nobody can say that you have no class.

I strongly advise against telling anyone to kiss your a%$. Wouldn't it be awful if ever someone smiled politely and proceeded to kiss you gently on the lips?

Hugging your child tightly until they stop crying (even though you've started)...priceless.

I never understood people who constantly proclaimed their love. I figured your relationship would speak for itself. If you have to tell me you are in love, it must not be as good as you say.

But now I get it. When you are truly madly in love and happy, you cannot contain it; there is an overwhelming need to share it.

Now, I'm one of the people constantly proclaiming love, annoying those who don't quite get it ... yet

Take care the heart of another. Once broken, it can never love the same.

All alone ~
I could be blue -
Instead, I choose to think of you ...
And I smile

Very soon ~
You will be home -
Then I no more will be alone ...
And I smile

Life is good ~
In fact, it's grand -
Cause we walk through it, hand in hand ...
And we smile

Those who say, "I wish my dog could talk" have never had a talking dog. (Good point, Troy!)

Your missing arm does not diminish the pain of my broken one. Why must we one-up each other's successes, failures, pain, and joy? Where is the gain? Sure, misery may love company, but I would far rather spend every Friday night home alone than to accept that party invite.

Ever had an entire discussion in your head, just to avoid having it with the person you should?

I like to write! Big shock, as you are currently reading a compilation of my writings. Following is a little ditty that crossed my mind during the wedding planning process. See if you can guess the iconic musical that inspired these words.

Cardstock, embossing and monogrammed letters;
cake tasting and designing (we did it together),
choosing the flowers and picking out rings
these are a few wedding planning things!

If you are concerned that the wrong person might hear what you are saying, perhaps you are confused about the part that is wrong.

Ignoring problems will not make them go away. On the other hand, ignoring people ...

Those who lie to ensure their success often find that they have ensured their failure.

What makes me sure I am with "the one"?

We have never asked each other to change because we love and accept each other exactly the way we are. We have traveled similar roads and recognize the road dust each other brings.

We do not rely on each other for happiness; we each enhance the happiness the other brought to the table.

We do not look to the other to save us and make us whole people, we brought complete (though not perfect) people to the relationship. We can just "be." Be who we are, with the one who loves us as we are.

I know in my "knower" that this is the one in part BECAUSE I have had failed relationships, and I know this is different. I know that I am with the one I can trust with my heart. Someone who will tell me deep and meaningful truths even when they are hard to hear. Someone who is proud to be with me but doesn't have to show me off. Someone who wrapped his arms around me and whispered, "You can trust me, you can love me, your heart is safe with me."

If she's not your Valentine every day, don't bother with a card on February 14th. The only one you will be fooling is yourself.

I do not have to be brilliant. I only need to be smarter than those I must outthink.

When you ask a question that begins with, "What kind of person … ?" You already have the answer in mind.

You know you are in love when: You watch a television show or read a story where a couple is in love, and one of them has a short time to live. You cry like a baby because you cannot imagine life without the one you love.

Sometimes people in your life who love you will disappoint you. Once you know that, when it happens, they will be meeting (rather than failing to meet) your expectations. Just a minor perspective shift makes some things easier to process.

Love is a word without adequate definition. How do you capture the smile that sneaks across your lips when you think about the one you love? The way your heart races when you are going for a visit, or awaiting his/her return? How the sound of their voice makes all the stress in life suddenly more manageable? And a hug, a hug makes you safe.

Love? No words are adequate because love is about trust, feelings, vulnerability, and on and on.

Thanksgiving makes me ever mindful of the human turkeys in my life.

Why seek external approval? Set your own bar; chart your own course.

Out of context quote: If dogs built chairs, they would look like ottomans.

Note to Hollywood: Love does not mean never having to say you're sorry (one of the most annoying lines ever). Love means being sincere when you say you are sorry, and setting about changing the behavior for which you are apologizing. Just my 82 cents.

If you don't like your reality, change it. Don't lie about it (to yourself, or anyone else).

Don't allow your fears to build a wall that separates you from happiness.

Don't go to bed angry. You will not be able to sleep. Your anger will fester. When you can address the issue in the morning, it will be a much larger issue because it has grown overnight. Don't go to bed angry.

Love is patient. Love is kind.

Love has a sense of humor and a sense of compassion.

Love is not oblivious to your flaws but allows you to think it is.

Love knows that alone life is good, but when loving and being equally loved, life is astounding, amazing, joyous beyond measure.

Love is - everything.

Sometimes, all we need is a good hug from someone who knows us completely and loves us still.

Dwelling on the past makes it impossible to live in the present.

Say "I love you" to the ones you love. Keeping it to yourself benefits no one.

Choose to be happy in spite of, not because of, your circumstances. You will have experiences regardless of your attitude, but your attitude can help shape the experience.

Live each day to the fullest, experience all you can so that when you die your "to do" list has few checkmarks but your "to live" list has no empty boxes.

In the blink of an eye, it's over.

Boy to Girl: I'm out of the *Knight in Shining Armor* business.

Girl to Boy: No worries, I'm nobody's *Damsel in Distress.*

I have decided to stop trying to explain the unexplainable, understand the irrational or make sense of the senseless.

I realize that I cannot control the actions of others, but I will no longer allow the actions of others to control me.

Taking care of yourself is a job you cannot afford to outsource.

True friendship is both a soft place to land when life is difficult, and a rock thrown hard at your head when you do something stupid. Followed by a ride to the hospital.

When someone else's knowledge and innovation threaten you, it is you who needs to change.

How sick are dogs, typically? Trying to decide whether I'm as sick as one (before I call my employer).

Guard the self-esteem of others as you would the well-being of a newborn. Do not tear others down, and do not stand idly by while someone else does.

You do not need anyone's permission to be awesome.

Some people only know how to have Love/Hate relationships. They love to hate. Sad, but true.

Looking at my to-do list and wondering why "rest" and "pamper myself" are nowhere to be found. Going to have to talk to the author.

Looking at my to-do list and wondering why "rest" and "pamper myself" are nowhere to be found. Going to have to talk to the author.

The fact that you have the right to do something does not make it the right thing to do.

Have you noticed that often the people who say, "I don't need to be told to do X" are the very ones who, in fact, *need* to be told (sometimes, repeatedly)?

Circumstances are created, not dictated.

No matter how much perfume you put on a pig, in the end, it still smells like bacon.

And just like the crisp, sweet smell of the air after a light spring rain, your love makes me believe that anything is possible.

Do not measure your success against the success of others. Rather, measure your success against your goals.

Your pets are at your mercy, but they should not need it if you love them as much and as unconditionally as they love you.

Choosing to be passive with regard to your negative circumstances is not the same as making a sacrifice. One is noble, the other...

Gratitude requires the absence of a sense of entitlement.

Taking the high road is a good thing. Just be careful to ensure that you don't fall off the cliff.

When one is inspired, one is more likely to be inspirational.

I find the rain strangely comforting, even when I do not need to be comforted.

We tend to fear losing most, that which we are not certain we deserve.

Misery may love company but so does happiness. Come, stand in the sunshine with me.

It's not that I think it is bad to be you … it's just that I know how great it is to be me.

While it is important to have people in your life who tell you what a good, considerate, smart (insert positive attribute here) person you are – it is far more important that you know it to be true, without being told.

The key is to look at yourself in the mirror and like the inner reflection that you see.

9/11

The one day we grieve for those we have never met, as though they are family. Because for one day each year, everyone is family. Would that it lasted longer than one day.

Choices we make, good or bad, alter our course. Sometimes we barely notice, other times the change is drastic and lifelong. Not liking where your choices have taken you – does not change where you are. You cannot go back in time and undo your choices. Grow up, own up, man or woman up -- and start making the choices that move you closer to the goals you now know you want to achieve.

When you put yourself in a box, it is all the harder to think outside it.

When there is no one to count on but yourself, you begin to realize how strong, resourceful and capable you are. You learn how to stand your ground, fight for what you believe in, accept responsibility and crave growth. Because of this, when you finally have someone else to count on (s)he will know (s)he can also count on you.

When you are comfortable (dare I say, happy even) with who you are ... then you are not threatened by who anyone else is.

I do not determine what is right for me based on other people's successes, failures, standards, morals (or the lack thereof), or work ethic. What is right for me is what makes me proud of myself, and what lets me sleep at night. I do not owe anyone an explanation of my choices. So long as I would either make the same choice again or have learned a valuable lesson from an error in judgment ... I am happy.

Some people do not know how good they have it until it is gone; others, how bad. A wise man once said, "Sometimes you become absurd to survive absurd." Here's to no more absurdity!

Even those closest to you will not always share your opinions. That is perfectly OK, so long as they respect your right to have them.

Sometimes, life feels a bit overwhelming, busy, demanding. It can seem like I am no longer in control, just along for the ride. In those moments, I look at the two amazing people (and ridiculously cute dogs, and equally cute guinea pig) I share a home with, and realize that these are the important things, this is what it is about ... and it is all good.

I am stretched so thin you would think I'd be, well, thinner!

I am worth taking risks for, being honest with, and being loved as fiercely as I love. I know that while everything doesn't necessarily happen for a reason, everything certainly happens. I am strong, courageous, loving, compassionate and wise enough to weather any storm; and to fully, excitedly and unabashedly treasure the rainbows!

The only person your words teach anyone about is you.

It truly is wanting what you have vs. having what you want. Life is a series of setting goals and reaching them or failing to reach them and learning from the experience. In the meantime, embracing where you are "at the moment" is every bit as fulfilling as reaching the next goal.

Life is exactly as good, or as bad, as you judge it to be right here, right now.

When things always seem to "work themselves out" … perhaps that's karma.

Do not share your progress with those who can only celebrate perfection.

Careful, lest the judgments you pass on others burn a bridge that your forgiveness cannot rebuild.

Every day is an opportunity to reinvent yourself. If you do not like who you were yesterday, own it, and become more of the person you want to be today. If you have damaged relationships, do your best to repair the damage. Do not dwell on your past, instead, work toward a better future.

It is a lot easier to be "holier than thou" when there is no real likelihood that you will find yourself being a "thou."

Integrity? Honesty in the face of peer pressure, and at the cost of popularity, is a true testament to character.

Some people are so focused on what could have been, that they are unable to see what can still be.

Something about the holidays makes the world feel smaller, less self-centered, full of hope and promise.

"You can't fire me because I quit!" "You can't leave me, because I'm leaving you!" Interesting that some people think saying something is not so, it somehow becomes "not so." Reminds me of the schoolyard mentality that says, "I know you are, but what am I?"

Something about the holidays makes the world feel smaller, less self-centered, full of hope and promise.

It is not true that opportunity only knocks once. Like any good paper route collector, it will come back when it is certain you are home. The question is, will you answer the door?

Sometimes, "Objects in the mirror are more difficult than they appear."

Life is a daily lesson. Sometimes the school of hard knocks has to whack you on the head before you figure out how to make an ice pack.

When the new man in your daughter's life, who is much older than she, is a horse;

When she would rather spend her time riding and literally "shoveling sh*t" — than spend her money on the latest fad;

When you can tell she is happier at the barn than at the mall, or happier at a horse show than a concert...that is priceless!

If contemplation leads to revelation, that is a good thing. If courage acts on that revelation, that is a great thing.

When your gut tells you something that your brain tries to talk you out of, trust your gut. Your gut does not care what other people think, or even what you think; it just knows what it knows.

If people redirected the energy they spend being angry, and instead did something positive for someone else; they would be better for it. The world would be better for it.

Dang! These glasses make my dress look too small!

Do something right now that will move you closer to making your dream a reality.

When someone else wishes they had what you have, receive it as a compliment. Your happiness and success are tangible, and sadly, sometimes that makes others more aware of how unhappy they find themselves. Perhaps instead of huffing off at the audacity, you can be a mentor. Sometimes, the only thing standing between a person and the life they want is having been told they aren't capable of or don't deserve, better.

Sometimes, no matter how hard you try to come up with good reasons for someone's poor choices, there simply are none. And no matter how many times you tell yourself that it doesn't bother you, it does.

Every once in a while, it is important to say, "I love you" to the person looking at you in the mirror.

The fact that someone won't stop being a bully doesn't mean that you can't stop being their victim.

If you are asking yourself why you always seem to be playing the part of fool...consider that you gave the best audition for the role, and your failure to accept responsibility keeps you typecast.

The words "you are amazing" are not always meant as a compliment.

You do not possess the ability to control other people. Realizing this, ask yourself why you give others the ability to control you.

I am making a conscious change in perspective. Everything and everyone, work, school and activities outside the house are all part of my life because I have invited them in. Therefore, my life is not "busy" – it is "full" – and I am grateful.

When someone has "ripped" abs, we call that a six pack. If they have a great behind, do we call that a fanny pack?

Encourage others. A moment out of your life could be the turning point in someone else's.

The wisdom of a child: "You should never use the bathroom at a buffet restaurant. You might walk in on something that will make you lose your appetite then you wasted all that money."

Hero worship always feels better when you are the hero.

I am aware that not everyone thinks the way I do. That's OK; I forgive them.

Dear Karma,

Why do you have to be such a chameleon?

Yours Truly,
The Other Shoe

If it is true that you must play the hand dealt to you, perhaps it is best to learn how to count cards (or start flirting with the dealer).

Ode to the Weekend~

Friday, I love you,
when the workday is done
I rush home to family
and start having fun.

We laugh, and we joke,
we run here and there
we behave just like children
who don't have a care.

We spend time with family,
we spend time with friends
counting the hours
'til we meet again.

Steps to Sanity

1: Recognize that I am only one person.

2: Only agree to do things that I will not resent doing.

3: Understand that I am in as much need of my care and concern as anyone else.

4: Ask for help when I need it.

5: Expect others to accept "not at this time" without it damaging our relationship, rather than fearing the opposite.

6: Realize that while I DO wear tights from time to time ... I am NOT a superhero.

7: Be at peace with steps 1-6.

8: Rinse and repeat.

You make time for what is important to you. Look at your calendar for the next 30 days: Are there more "must do" items than "want to do" items? How much time did you schedule for friends and family?

Try color-coding, so you can instantly see where you are spending most of your time. If there is not enough of the color designated for friends/family, it is time to do some rescheduling.

If I could change one thing about myself, it would be … my shoes. This pair is slightly uncomfortable. Yep, most definitely the shoes!

One day, I'm going to say the things I've always wished I could say but was too worried about what others would think. When that day comes, nobody will be left to wonder "is this the day?"

Choose to be happy. It is much better for everyone.

When your happiness is measured and increased in direct proportion to how much its very existence will upset someone else, there is a real problem. You will find it by looking in the mirror.

The world is full of people who are all too happy to put limits on your success. Don't volunteer to do it for them. When you reach for more than you are capable of, you stretch and grow and become the person you are striving to be.

When you are facing someone who is determined to rain on your parade, decide to be OK with getting wet!

He who makes a punchline of others often becomes the joke.

Life is not a game, so there is no sense keeping score. When you wake up each day determined that it will be better than the day before, you are already a winner.

Even the famous label-making company figured out that labels should not be permanent. They make a good deal of money selling removable labels. This can be applied to life as well:

Don't let others permanently label you. Peel off their label and set about defining yourself.

When someone questions my stance on something, it does not threaten me; it enlightens me. Sometimes to holes in my thinking, sometimes to holes in their character.

I never wanted a career as a counselor because I was afraid I would carry other people's burdens home. It never occurred to me that I could help them learn to carry their burdens until they could lay them down and walk away. It seems that I am frequently able to do just that.

Believing that you are the only person with the right to an opinion (or worse, that yours is the only opinion that is right) is the height of both ignorance and arrogance.

"If you don't like your life, change it," they said. So she did. It was then they realized they wanted to change their lives, and they asked her to help.

When nothing is working *for* you, perhaps *you* are working *against yourself.*

Sometimes I find myself sticking to a way of thinking because challenging my thinking feels like challenging my integrity, or my intelligence. The truth is: We can only learn when we make ourselves teachable.

Dreams become a reality not because of the dream, but because of the dreamer.

Those who are not happy with themselves are rarely happy for others. Do not take it personally.

Do you have a reason for reaching your goal, or are you too busy making excuses for not reaching it?

When it is necessary to tear others down to build yourself up, perhaps it is time to consider a change in building materials.

Destructive criticism typically disguises itself as constructive feedback.

When a person diminishes your worth out loud, consider that they have already diminished their own in silence.

When a person cannot see your value, chances are they were blinded to their own long ago.

When a person cannot see your value, chances are they were blinded to their own long ago.

You do not have to control the waters; you only have to navigate them.

Expectation allows for disappointment while the lack of expectation allows for surprise.

When somebody does something for you, but they do it differently than you would the appropriate response is, "Thank you."

When you are looking up at a mountain that you must climb, there are at least two positives:

1. Good Exercise
2. Great View

Climb the mountain. It is the only way to get out of the valley.

Love does not mean accepting someone's worst, simply because they refuse to give you their best.

The most important relationship you will ever have is the one with yourself. If you do not love and accept yourself, there will always be a wall between you and every other person in your life.

The fastest, most effective way to ensure you never achieve your goals is to stop pursuing them!

It's perfectly OK to say "I told you so" – so long as what you told them was:

- You can do it
- You are capable
- I have faith in you
- I am here for you
- You've got this

When your heart is breaking, your mind often jumps in trying to make sense of the pain so the healing can begin. Sometimes, your heart needs to tell your mind to back off. There is no sense to be made of the senseless, only pain that must be felt fully to heal fully.

If you treated yourself the way you treat others, would your self-care be better, or worse?

Just because you are not someone's cup of tea, does not mean you should try to figure out how to be coffee. Be you. Authentically – Relentlessly – Unapologetically You! Those who like the kind of tea you are will never find you if you are busy trying to be coffee.

Don't let other people's failures put limits on your success.

I'm OK with me. So much so, that I'm also ok if you are not ok with me.

Sometimes the right thing is not easy. Sometimes the easy thing is not right. Integrity does not recognize hard or easy, only right.

If it is important to you, it is important, period. Do not allow the opinions of others to make you question whether something should matter. If it ever mattered to you, it matters, period.

We create our truth by believing it. If we believe the lies (self-doubt) we tell ourselves, they will become our truth.

When you truly open your heart to another; you give them the power to break you, and trust that they won't.

The best thing the voice in my head ever said to me: "I forgive you."

ABOUT THE AUTHOR (THAT'S ME)

I am an author, an obstacle crusher, and a spark igniter. Part advice columnist, part motivational speaker, and champion for those who are ready to overcome fear, eliminate excuses, and have "drive-by epiphanies" that throat punch mediocrity.

A lover of all things motivational, inspirational and thought-provoking, it is not surprising that this would be the focus of my first book.

I am wife to a man I met in high school; quirky mom to an equally quirky daughter; poetry, and prose writing fiend; an acceptable vocalist, dreadful at anything requiring hand-eye coordination and a confidence cultivator.

I believe that…
- Often the only thing standing in our way is the reflection in the mirror.
- When a person mixes confidence with action, the result is always amazing.
- Nobody who bought a Y2K survival kit got a refund; and, whoever came up with the idea was a genius.

Bonus! Increase your confidence and improve your outlook in just 5 minutes a day using proven Mindset Mini Mantras
My gift to you at: www.wisdomwitandwhimsy.com/bookbonus

www.ingramcontent.com/pod-product-compliance
Lightning Source LLC
Chambersburg PA
CBHW061152040426
42445CB00013B/1661